CW01082747

Original title:

Embracing Intimacy

Author: Kätriin Kaldaru

ISBN HARDBACK: 978-9916-89-100-1

ISBN PAPERBACK: 978-9916-89-101-8

ISBN EBOOK: 978-9916-89-102-5

Illuminated Hearts

In shadows deep, we find the light,
A spark ignites, a brave new sight.
Hearts entwined in gentle grace,
Together we dance, a timeless space.

Through laughter shared and whispers low,
Each secret shared makes our love grow.
With every glance, our souls combine,
Two hearts as one, in love we shine.

Navigating the Depths

In ocean's sway, we drift and glide,
The currents pull, we take the ride.
Beneath the waves, the mysteries lie,
We dive with hope beneath the sky.

With every stroke, we find our course,
In depths unknown, we feel the force.
The tides may change, but we hold tight,
Our hearts aligned, we face the night.

A Canvas of Silences

In quiet hues, emotions play,
Each whispered word, a soft ballet.
Our dreams unfold in shimmering shades,
Where silence speaks, and light invades.

Brushstrokes blend in perfect time,
A masterpiece crafted, a silent rhyme.
In every pause, a story's spun,
A canvas of love, a world begun.

Moments Between Heartbeats

In fleeting time, we pause to breathe,
A heartbeat shared, we dare to believe.
Between each pulse, our dreams ignite,
In sacred spaces, love takes flight.

The world may blur, yet here we stand,
Each moment quick, yet filled and grand.
A gentle touch, a gaze so sweet,
In heartbeats' dance, our souls compete.

In the Warmth of Familiarity

In the quiet corners, we reside,
Whispers of memories, a gentle guide.
Hands intertwined, hearts at ease,
In the warmth of familiarity, we seize.

Each sunset paints a story anew,
With laughter echoing, soft and true.
Days weave together, threads so fine,
In the warmth of our bond, we shine.

Every shared glance, a spark ignites,
Bringing comfort to lonely nights.
With every heartbeat, a dance unfolds,
In the warmth of familiarity, love beholds.

Through storms we weather, side by side,
In moments of silence, with hearts open wide.
We cherish the stillness, the joy, the pain,
In the warmth of familiarity, we gain.

In seasons that change, we stand as one,
In the golden glow of the setting sun.
Together we flourish, forever entwined,
In the warmth of familiarity, love defined.

The Fragrance of Shared Laughter

In gardens where joy does bloom,
The fragrance of laughter fills the room.
With each quick smile and playful jest,
Together we find our hearts at rest.

Moments like petals, light and bright,
We gather them close, a pure delight.
Echoes of giggles, a melody sweet,
The fragrance of laughter, our hearts' retreat.

Stories unfold under starry skies,
With each shared tale, a bond that ties.
In the dance of shadows, we take our chance,
In the fragrance of laughter, we dance.

Time slips away but we stay near,
Each shared whisper, a treasure dear.
In the warmth of the moment, we find our way,
In the fragrance of laughter, we stay.

The world may change, but we remain,
In the joyful echoes, love's refrain.
Together we bloom, wherever we roam,
In the fragrance of laughter, we're home.

The Depths We Find Together

In the depths of our souls, we explore,
Uncharted waters, we both adore.
With every dive, we discover grace,
In the depths we find our sacred space.

The waves may crash, the tides may turn,
But in this journey, we will learn.
Side by side, we brave the storm,
In the depths, our spirits warm.

Secrets shared, like treasures deep,
In the quiet moments, love we keep.
With open hearts, we dare to tread,
In the depths, our fears are shed.

Each heartbeat echoes, a rhythmic flow,
In this vast ocean, together we grow.
Through currents strong, we find our song,
In the depths we belong, where we're strong.

Together we rise, through dark and light,
In the depths of love, we shine bright.
Forever anchored, where dreams tether,
In the depths we find ourselves together.

Breath to Breath

Inhale the dawn's soft glow,
Each sigh a whisper of hope.
Exhale the shadows that linger,
Find solace in the quiet flow.

Moments dance in the silence,
Like ripples on a still lake.
Time flows gently, unhurried,
With memories we gently make.

The world spins fast around us,
Yet here, time holds its breath.
We weave our dreams together,
In the calm of love's depth.

Through twilight's tender embrace,
Stars awaken in our eyes.
Every heartbeat syncs like music,
Together under vast skies.

As twilight fades to darkness,
We cherish each shared sigh.
Breath to breath, heart to heart,
In love, we dare to fly.

We Unfold

Petals bloom in the morning light,
Each layer whispers a story.
In the garden of our joining,
We blossom in shared glory.

Time gently carves our edges,
With each laugh, with each tear.
We shed the weight of our questions,
Embracing the joy we hear.

Like rivers merging in the night,
We flow into one another.
Every secret, every dream,
Unraveled like a soft tether.

With every breath we take,
The world outside fades away.
In this space, we discover,
The beauty in our play.

Together we rise, we stand,
Unfolding with grace and care.
Bound by threads of trust and hope,
In love, we find our air.

Through the Prism of Togetherness

Light refracts in our laughter,
Colors dance in fleeting rays.
In this spectrum of our love,
We find joy in simple ways.

Every moment a canvas,
Painted in hues of delight.
Shadows mingle with brilliance,
Creating our world so bright.

Through the lens of our vision,
Together we weave our dreams.
Seeing life through our union,
More vibrant than it seems.

With hands clasped tight in trust,
We navigate the shine and dark.
Through the prism of togetherness,
Every spark ignites our spark.

In the melody of our hearts,
A symphony sweetly plays.
Together, forever, we shine,
In the dance of endless days.

Heartstrings Tied in Whispers

Softly tied with threads of gold,
Our hearts whisper tales of old.
In the silence, we find meaning,
Love's story gently untold.

Every glance a silent promise,
Every touch a secret share.
In the stillness of our moments,
We weave magic in the air.

Beneath the stars, we linger,
Tracing constellations bright.
In the warmth of connection,
We find our way through the night.

Whispers flutter like soft wings,
Carried on the winds of fate.
Heartstrings play a gentle tune,
In love's embrace, we create.

With each word softly spoken,
We build bridges to the soul.
Together, forever entwined,
In whispers, we are whole.

Navigating the Depths of Us

In the ocean of our being,
Waves crash softly on the shore.
We chart the depths and currents,
Finding treasures we adore.

With every heartbeat guiding,
We dive into the unknown.
In the silence, we discover,
The beauty of love's tone.

Together we swim through shadows,
With lanterns lighting our way.
In the depths of our connection,
We find our hearts' gentle sway.

The tides may rise and tumble,
Yet we balance with each flow.
In the dance of life and love,
We learn just where to go.

Through the depths we rise, we thrive,
Exploring vast, hidden seas.
Navigating the currents,
Together, we sail with ease.

Under the Veil of Night's Caress

The moon whispers soft and low,
Stars twinkle in a gentle flow.
Darkness wraps in warm embrace,
Secrets linger in this space.

The breeze carries tales untold,
While shadows dance, brave and bold.
Each rustle speaks of hidden dreams,
Underneath the silver beams.

Night blooms with a silent grace,
In stillness, we find our place.
The world outside fades away,
As we linger, night turns to day.

With every heartbeat, time suspends,
In the twilight, where love transcends.
Together, bound by fate's design,
Under the night, your hand in mine.

The stars above start to wane,
Yet in our hearts, love remains.
As dawn creeps in with its light,
We'll hold onto the warmth of night.

The Language of Unspoken Bonds

In glances shared, words float by,
A silent truth beneath the sky.
Hearts converse in fleeting stares,
Emotions knit through gentle airs.

Moments linger, thick with meaning,
Each unsaid thought, softly leaning.
In the quiet, we connect,
No need for words to interject.

A smile exchanged, a sigh released,
In this stillness, we find peace.
The bond we share, a hidden thread,
Woven deep in what's unsaid.

Through every trial, hand in hand,
Understanding grows, a quiet band.
In the spaces, trust takes form,
In our hearts, love's steady norm.

Each heartbeat finds its rhythm true,
Speaking volumes, just me and you.
Together in the silence's embrace,
We've built a world, our sacred space.

Threads Woven into the Fabric of Us

In every tapestry we create,
Threads of laughter, love, and fate.
Colors blend with every hue,
Each fiber tells a tale of you.

Moments stitched in memory's seam,
Woven closely, like a dream.
The fabric of our bond grows strong,
In every note, a timeless song.

With each challenge, we entwine,
In struggles faced, our hearts align.
A pattern rich in shared delight,
Crafted gently, day and night.

The weaver's hand, both kind and wise,
Beneath the surface, love never lies.
In every tear, a lesson learned,
In every joy, our passion burned.

Together, we'll spin tales anew,
Each thread a promise, tried and true.
In the tapestry of what we've spun,
Forever united, two become one.

In the Shadows, We Find Light

Within the dark, a flicker glows,
In shadowed corners, courage grows.
Though fear may linger close at hand,
A spark ignites, together we stand.

The hidden paths we dare to tread,
Illuminated by what's unsaid.
In quiet moments, strength we glean,
Finding beauty in the unseen.

With whispered hopes, we chase the night,
In every struggle, we seek the light.
Together, we brave the unknown sky,
Hand in hand, we learn to fly.

As dawn approaches, shadows wane,
Yet through the trials, we remain.
For in the depths of darkest plight,
We unearth joy, embracing light.

No longer bound by fear's dark call,
In unity, we rise, we fall.
In shadows deep, our hearts ignite,
Together, weaving day from night.

Moments that Linger Like Breath

In the hush of twilight's glow,
Memories dance, soft and slow.
Whispers weave through the night air,
Capturing laughter, beyond compare.

Each sigh a tale, untold and deep,
In gentle corners, secrets keep.
Time bends softly, allowing us,
To savor each moment, without rush.

In the warmth where shadows play,
We gather echoes of yesterday.
Threads of joy in every embrace,
Lingering echoes, time can't erase.

Every heartbeat reflects the light,
Illuminating the darkest night.
As dawn breaks, we hold it tight,
Moments that linger, pure delight.

The Warmth of Togetherness

In the glow of flickering flame,
Togetherness calls, never the same.
Hands intertwined, strength renewed,
In every glance, love is imbued.

We share the silence, the gentle peace,
In your presence, all worries cease.
The world outside fades to a hum,
In this cocoon, two hearts become.

Voices blend like a perfect song,
In this embrace, we both belong.
Moments passed, but never lost,
In love's embrace, we count the cost.

The laughter echoes, fills the air,
Each shared smile, a treasure rare.
With every heartbeat, time stands still,
In warm togetherness, we find our will.

Crossing Boundaries of the Soul

In the depths where shadows intertwine,
We dance on edges, your heart and mine.
No barriers can shield the glow,
Of souls entwined, as currents flow.

Each whispered truth, a bridge we build,
With every story shared, we're thrilled.
In the vast expanse, we break the mold,
Unlocking secrets, daring and bold.

In this realm, we ride the waves,
Healing wounds, our hearts like braves.
With gentle steps, we venture on,
Finding light at each break of dawn.

The silence speaks in vibrant hues,
In each connection, we choose our views.
Through the layers, we dive so deep,
Crossing boundaries, our dreams we keep.

Caress of Trust in the Silence

In the quiet night where whispers cease,
A caress of trust brings our hearts peace.
Words unspoken, yet understood,
In this silence, we find our good.

The softest gaze holds worlds unknown,
In each moment, seeds of love are sown.
Every heartbeat resonates, so pure,
In this stillness, our souls endure.

Together we tread, on paths refined,
In the caress of trust, our lives aligned.
Beneath the starlit sky, we stand,
In unity, we craft our strand.

Every sigh, a promise made,
In the warmth of silence, fears will fade.
Bonded deeply, through thick and thin,
In the caress of trust, we begin.

Fragile Moments of Unity

In the quiet of dawn, we stand,
Whispers dance between our hands.
Glances shared, words left unsaid,
Together here, where hope is bred.

With laughter woven in our breath,
We cherish life, we conquer death.
Fragile threads that bind us tight,
In this moment, pure and bright.

Time may bend, but we hold strong,
Creating memories, where we belong.
In silence, love begins to grow,
In fragile moments, truth will flow.

The world may tremble, storms may rage,
Yet here we write our sacred page.
In unity, our spirits twine,
Connected hearts, your beat with mine.

So let us dance through fleeting days,
In harmony's soft, gentle ways.
Together we'll face what lies ahead,
In fragile moments, love is spread.

When Hearts Speak in Rhythm

In twilight's grace, our souls align,
With every breath, our hearts entwine.
In silent beats, the world will fade,
When hearts speak, love's serenade.

A gentle touch, a knowing glance,
Together lost in a shared dance.
Melody hums, the night alive,
In perfect sync, our spirits thrive.

Words may falter, but beats remain,
Through joy and sorrow, through pleasure and pain.
In every thump, we find our way,
When hearts speak, night turns to day.

Each pulse a promise, strong and clear,
We journey onward, year to year.
In rhythms deep, we find our home,
When hearts speak, we're never alone.

So let the music guide our path,
As we embrace love's gentle wrath.
Together we rise, come what may,
When hearts speak, we will stay.

An Invitation to the Depths

Beneath the surface, shadows play,
An ocean vast calls us to stay.
With sparkling waves, secrets unfold,
An invitation to hearts so bold.

In the stillness, depths reveal,
What lies beneath, a sacred seal.
Hold my hand, let's dive anew,
In the dark, I'll search for you.

With every current, fears will sway,
And in these depths, we'll find our way.
We'll navigate through the unknown,
In shadows' edge, love has grown.

Together we'll find treasures rare,
In the abyss, our souls laid bare.
An invitation to deeper grace,
In trust and love, we find our place.

So take this plunge, don't hesitate,
Embrace the depths, set hearts straight.
Together we'll explore what's true,
An invitation, just me and you.

Rapture in the In-Between

Where silence blooms and shadows kiss,
In moments caught, we find our bliss.
Between the words, the laughter flows,
In rapture's grip, our love just grows.

The space between each heart's desire,
Ignites our souls, sets hearts afire.
In glances shared, in quiet sighs,
We craft the dreams where passion lies.

What's left unsaid, a sweet embrace,
In every pause, we find our place.
A tender touch, the world slows down,
In rapture's hold, we both are found.

So dance with me in this sweet pause,
In every beat, our hearts find cause.
For life's best moments, soft and keen,
Are rapture found in the in-between.

Together we weave through time and space,
In gentle blends, we find our grace.
In stillness, love's true meaning gleans,
In rapture's light, we're ever seen.

Trails of Connection Through Time

We wander paths of memory,
Where shadows dance in sunlit haze.
Each step we take, a history,
With whispers echoing our days.

Beneath the trees that witnessed growth,
Our laughter stitched through woven air.
In every glance, an honest oath,
To cherish moments always rare.

These trails we walk, they intertwine,
Like vines that clasp the oakwood's heart.
Together here, our lives align,
A tapestry, each thread a part.

The seasons shift, yet still we roam,
Through fields of gold and skies of gray.
With every journey leading home,
Our souls like rivers find their way.

As time extends its hands to us,
We grasp the now and let it flow.
In every smile, a silent trust,
For love ignites what we both know.

When Eyes Speak Volumes

In silence, words can softly land,
Where gazes meet and stories thrive.
A glance can show what hearts have planned,
And in their depths, true feelings dive.

When laughter sparkles in the air,
Or sorrow pools like still, dark seas,
The eyes unveil what hearts lay bare,
Their language flows like whispered pleas.

A moment holds, the world stands still,
With just a glance, a tale unfolds.
Through eyes that shine, we feel the thrill,
Of secret thoughts and dreams retold.

In crowded rooms, we find our peace,
Through fleeting looks, connections bloom.
In every blink, our souls release,
The truths that flourish in the gloom.

So let your gaze be ever bright,
For in those depths, love's shadows play.
In every look, a pure delight,
As hearts converse in silent sway.

Emblazoned in Soft Light

The dawn unfolds in hues of gold,
As whispers wrap the waking world.
Each ray a story yet untold,
In tender arms, our dreams unfurled.

The evening glows with warm embrace,
As twilight paints the sky in rose.
In every shadow, there's a trace,
Of love that through the ages flows.

When stars ignite, the night extends,
A canvas vast with cosmic art.
In every twinkle, time transcends,
And lights the pathways of the heart.

Embraced by dusk, we softly sway,
Our hopes reflected in the dark.
In every glow, we find our way,
With flickering lights, we leave our mark.

As morning breaks, anew we rise,
With soft light warming every breath.
In every dawn, the promise lies,
Of love that conquers even death.

In the Garden of Our Shared Space

Among the blooms of vivid hue,
We nurture dreams beneath the sun.
In whispered winds, our wishes grew,
And in this haven, we are one.

With every seed, a story sown,
As roots entwine in soil so deep.
Together here, we've always known,
Our love's a promise we will keep.

The gentle rain, it bathes our souls,
Each droplet sparkles with delight.
In this lush realm, our passion rolls,
A symphony of day and night.

In quiet corners, laughter rings,
As blossoms sway in joyous dance.
In harmony, our spirit sings,
A melody that holds a trance.

So in this garden, let us stay,
With hands entwined and hearts embraced.
Through time and space, we'll find our way,
In beauty's bloom, forever graced.

A Tapestry of Vulnerability

In shadows cast by whispered dreams,
We find a strength that softly gleams.
Fragile hearts in open view,
Together, we stitch a thread so true.

With every tear, a story spun,
A tapestry of lives well done.
In courage found in soft embrace,
We gather warmth in this shared space.

Each frayed edge speaks of our plight,
Yet, through the dark, we seek the light.
Unraveled truths are gently sewn,
In vulnerability, we've truly grown.

The threads may tangle, knots may rise,
Yet beauty lies in these fragile ties.
In every stitch, a bond we weave,
A testament to those who believe.

So here we stand, with hearts laid bare,
Embracing flaws, shedding despair.
In this fabric of shared despair,
Vulnerability's strength is found rare.

Secrets Wrapped in Serenity

In quiet whispers, secrets lay,
Beneath the stars, we find our way.
Wrapped in silence, stories kept,
In serene moments, doubts are swept.

A gentle breeze through trees will tell,
Of unspoken thoughts, we know too well.
In hidden nooks, where shadows dance,
We share our dreams in quiet glance.

Serenity cradles fragile fears,
In these sacred spaces, our hearts clear.
With every sigh, we lay things bare,
Secrets wrapped in tender care.

Trust, the fabric of our bond,
In silence deep, we respond.
For in these hushed, unveiled nights,
Our secrets soar on quiet flights.

The moonlight casts a gentle glow,
As we unearth what few may know.
In serenity's embrace, we find,
The peace of souls forever twined.

Echoes of Familiarity

In streets we walked, together found,
Echoes whisper, a distant sound.
Familiar paths that memories trace,
We share our laughter in time and space.

The scent of rain on asphalt streets,
Brings back the joy of simple feats.
In every smile, a tale retold,
Echoes linger as time unfolds.

Old songs play on the radio,
Carrying us where fondness flows.
In every note, a cherished face,
Familiar warmth brings us back to grace.

Through seasons change, we always meet,
In woven threads of hearts that beat.
Echoes of love, forever near,
In familiar corners, we persevere.

With hands entwined, we greet the dawn,
In shared moments, new bonds are drawn.
Together, we'll navigate life's seas,
With echoes of familiarity, we are at ease.

A Canvas of Kindred Spirits

On this canvas, colors blend,
Where stories meet and hearts transcend.
In strokes of laughter, tears in hues,
We paint our lives, each shade review.

With every brush, our spirits glow,
In vivid dreams, together flow.
Kindred hearts, a masterpiece,
In unity, our souls find peace.

Every line, a whispered thought,
In this union, hope is sought.
Together, we dream, weave, and mold,
A tapestry of hearts so bold.

As daylight fades, our art remains,
In every shadow, love sustains.
With palettes bright, we share our plight,
In kindred spirits, we find our light.

A canvas vast, we fill with grace,
In every touch, a warm embrace.
Together, we create an art,
A living testament of the heart.

In the Sanctuary of Two

In a world where whispers dwell,
Soft shadows dance, a secret spell.
Hand in hand, we find our peace,
In the sanctuary, fears release.

Through the noise, our hearts align,
In the stillness, love divine.
Every glance, a gentle touch,
In our refuge, we are so much.

Time drifts by, a tender breeze,
With you, my soul finds sweet ease.
In your eyes, the stars reside,
Together here, we can confide.

Promises wrapped in sacred light,
Echoes of laughter, pure delight.
In our haven, dreams take flight,
In this space, all feels right.

As days fade and the dusk draws near,
In our sanctuary, I hold you dear.
With every heartbeat, love will prove,
In the sanctuary of two, we move.

Glimmers of Soft Trust

In the dawn of morning's glow,
Gentle moments start to flow.
With every word, a bond is made,
In this dance, our fears will fade.

Eyes that meet, a silent vow,
In this space, we learn somehow.
Every heartbeat whispers true,
In this trust, I find you.

Through the shadows, light will creep,
In your arms, I fall so deep.
No more doubts, just endless grace,
In your love, I find my place.

Through the storms and skies of grey,
Glimmers of hope lead the way.
In the stillness, hand in hand,
Together here, we firmly stand.

As seasons change and years may fly,
With you, my heart learns to try.
In the whispers of the night,
Glimmers of soft trust, our light.

The Heart's Gentle Symphony

In the silence, music plays,
Each heartbeat sings in soft arrays.
With every note, our spirits soar,
In this harmony, we explore.

Strings of laughter, winds of grace,
In each moment, time we embrace.
Melodies weave through sunlit days,
In the rhythm, love stays ablaze.

Whispers linger, echoing light,
Through shadows deep, our souls unite.
The heart's soft song, a tender guide,
In this symphony, we confide.

As the world turns, a dance we find,
In the twilight, we're intertwined.
Each crescendo, a sweet release,
In this melody, we find peace.

Forever etched in twilight's call,
The heart's gentle symphony, our all.
With every breath, we learn to sing,
In this music, love takes wing.

In the Quiet, We Ignite

In the hush of evening's shade,
Soft moments bloom, unafraid.
With whispered dreams, we set the fire,
In quietude, our hearts aspire.

Stars above, a watchful gaze,
In stillness held, a tender phrase.
Every heartbeat fuels the flame,
In the quiet, love's wild game.

Hidden thoughts, now laid bare,
In this sacred space, we share.
Tender glances, sparks in flight,
In the quiet, we ignite.

Through the shadows, light will creep,
In your presence, my heart leaps.
Every sigh, a gentle breeze,
In this stillness, our souls seize.

As night unfolds and dreams take shape,
In our embrace, the world escapes.
Together here, passion's light,
In the quiet, we ignite.

The Comfort of Togetherness

In the warmth of shared glances,
We find peace in silent spaces.
Hands entwined, hearts aligned,
Together, we create our places.

Laughter dances in the air,
A symphony of joyful sounds.
In each moment, we declare,
Home is where love abounds.

Through storms and gentle rains,
We weather all that life brings.
In your eyes, I see the plains,
Of dreams where hope still sings.

Every sunset paints our sky,
With hues of memories past.
In your presence, I can fly,
A bond that forever lasts.

Together, we write our story,
With pages filled with light.
In the comfort, there's no worry,
For our hearts shine ever bright.

Caresses of Forgotten Dreams

In twilight's hush, whispers linger,
Soft echoes of what could be.
Fingers trace the air like fingers,
Reaching for lost reverie.

Sleepless nights bring tales to light,
Of hopes once held, now slipped away.
In shadows, we renew our sight,
Chasing dawns of yesterday.

Memories drift like clouds in flight,
Painting stories on our skin.
With every sigh, we ignite,
The flame that dwells within.

Yet still, the heart knows how to dream,
To weave the fabric of the past.
In silence, we hear it scream,
For love that's meant to last.

And with each dawn, we will rise,
Embrace the change that life redeems.
In every heartbeat, love replies,
To caresses of forgotten dreams.

Where Trust Blossoms

In the quiet of our hearts,
Seeds of trust begin to grow.
Nurtured by the gentle arts,
In the garden, love will sow.

Through honesty, roots we lay,
With openness, we build our walls.
In the light of each new day,
We flourish where the heart calls.

Every promise that we make,
Is a branch stretching toward the sky.
In this bond, we never break,
Our spirits learn to fly high.

Fears dissolve like morning mist,
As we share our deepest fears.
In each moment, love persists,
Woven strong through all the years.

Together, we face the unknown,
In trust, we find our way.
In this safe place, we have grown,
Where love and trust forever stay.

Pulses in Harmony

In the rhythm of our hearts,
A dance that knows no end.
With every beat, life imparts,
The joy that two can blend.

Steps entwined, we glide and sway,
In the music made for two.
In silence, we find our way,
Each moment feels so new.

Through the chaos, we create,
A song of love that won't disperse.
In the breath of each heartbeat,
We embrace the universe.

In the chorus of our souls,
We sing in vibrant hues.
With each pulse, the world unfolds,
A symphony of you.

Together, we write our score,
In harmony, we will soar.
With life's cadence evermore,
Our love, a song we'll adore.

Sharing Sacred Spaces

In quiet corners, hearts align,
Soft whispers float through the air,
Hand in hand, we intertwine,
A tapestry of love laid bare.

Reflecting light in gentle grace,
Moments paused in serene embrace,
Shared laughter fills the empty night,
In these spaces, souls take flight.

Echoes of dreams softly blend,
As time bends, and sorrows mend,
Nature's symphony hums along,
Together we craft a sacred song.

Through trials faced and joy to share,
We journey forth, bound by care,
Every heartbeat sings in rhyme,
In our shared horizon, we find time.

So here we stand, hearts open wide,
Embracing love, our constant guide,
In sharing spaces, we ignite,
A universe of pure delight.

Threads of Silent Understanding

In silence, we weave our tale,
Words unspoken gently trail,
A glance, a nod, a tender sigh,
In this stillness, we learn to fly.

Threads connect where hearts embrace,
A dance of trust in sacred space,
Moments linger, soft and slow,
In silent whispers, love will grow.

Through every glance, a world exists,
Language lost, yet still persists,
We grasp the heart of someone's truth,
Finding bonds, eternal youth.

Yet in the quiet, echoes bloom,
A depth of feeling dispels the gloom,
With every pause, we start anew,
In silence, we see the deeper view.

Together weaving dreams that shine,
A tapestry of souls entwined,
With threads so fine, our hearts expand,
In this realm, we understand.

When Shadows Dance Together

Beneath the moon's soft silver glow,
In twilight's embrace, shadows flow,
Fingers entwined, we find our way,
As laughter carries the night away.

Echoes of whispers, secrets shared,
In the dark, our love declared,
Painting dreams on a canvas wide,
In this moment, we won't divide.

With every step, the darkness light,
Shadows flicker, hearts ignite,
Lost in the rhythm of gentle sway,
In this dance, we find our play.

As stars above witness our grace,
We twirl and turn, they keep our pace,
In the quiet, our spirits blend,
Two shadows merging, love's true friend.

Together we'll roam, hand in hand,
In this world, we understand,
For when shadows dance and hearts soar,
We discover what love is for.

Close Enough to Breathe

In the stillness, we softly meet,
Hearts synchronizing, warm and sweet,
Breath to breath, a lullaby,
In your presence, I learn to fly.

Fingers trace the lines of fate,
In gentle moments, we celebrate,
The space between our souls so near,
In that closeness, everything's clear.

Eyes like oceans, deep and wide,
In quiet gazes, we confide,
Exhaling dreams, the world suspended,
In this warmth, all doubt's upended.

Whispers linger, time stands still,
In your gaze, I find my will,
Together woven, thread by thread,
In the silence, love is spread.

Close enough to breathe as one,
Two hearts united, life's begun,
In this embrace, we discover grace,
In every heartbeat, a sacred space.

A Tangle of Souls

In shadows deep, two hearts collide,
Threads entwined, we gently bide.
Whispers soft, secrets shared,
In this dance, we both are scared.

Moonlight glimmers on our paths,
Fates entwined in quiet wraths.
A tapestry of love and pain,
A beautiful storm, a sweet refrain.

Through the chaos, we find our way,
Guided by love's bright display.
Each heartbeat echoes, strong and loud,
In the silence, we stand proud.

With every tear, a lesson learned,
A fire ignites, our spirits burned.
Together we rise, through hills and valleys,
In this tangle, our love rallies.

In the end, when all is said,
Through tangled souls, we'll forge ahead.
Forever bound, no more to roam,
In this tangle, we've found our home.

The Quiet Symphony of Us

In silent rooms, we share a glance,
A melody born from our chance.
Notes of laughter fill the air,
In every moment, love we share.

Gentle whispers blend like dreams,
A symphony flows, or so it seems.
Hands together, fingers interlace,
In this music, we find our place.

Each heartbeat's rhythm, a soft refrain,
Carving echoes of joy and pain.
In the quiet, our souls align,
A perfect harmony, yours and mine.

Through every storm, we dance and sway,
With every note, we find our way.
Though life may play a different tune,
Together, we're a vibrant bloom.

As time unfolds, this song will grow,
A gentle symphony, a steady flow.
In whispered dreams, our hearts discuss,
The quiet beauty that is us.

Echoes of a Gentle Touch

In the stillness, your fingers trace,
A tender map, a soft embrace.
Every gesture whispers low,
Creating echoes, love's sweet flow.

Like autumn leaves that fall and sway,
Your touch ignites the fading day.
Moments linger, shadows cast,
In your warmth, I'm home at last.

With every sigh, a dream takes flight,
In your presence, the world feels right.
Gentle echoes fill the night,
Our hearts awake, in shared delight.

Time stands still as our hands explore,
A silent promise, forevermore.
Each heartbeat joins, a soothing song,
In this dance, where we belong.

As twilight fades, I'm filled with you,
A gentle touch that feels so true.
In every echo, love's sweet pain,
We find ourselves, in joy and rain.

In the Warmth of Our Embrace

In twilight's glow, we stand entwined,
A universe in you I find.
Soft breaths whisper like the breeze,
In the warmth, my heart finds ease.

The world outside fades to gray,
In your arms, I long to stay.
With every heartbeat, time does freeze,
Wrapped in warmth, I'm filled with peace.

Fingers laced, we dream awake,
Every promise, no mistake.
In this circle, love and grace,
Together lost, we find our space.

Through stormy nights and sunny days,
Your presence lights my darkest ways.
In the warmth of your embrace,
I've found my home, my sacred place.

As moments pass like whispered sighs,
In this haven, love never dies.
Forever bound, let time erase,
The world outside, in our embrace.

Layers of Touch in Starlight

Beneath the cosmic gaze we share,
A whisper floats through midnight air.
Gentle fingers, soft and warm,
Caress the night, a tender charm.

In shadows deep, our secrets spin,
Each heartbeat speaks where dreams begin.
Light drapes over fragile skin,
A tapestry of where we've been.

Through silver beams, our souls entwine,
In silence deep, the stars align.
With every brush, a story told,
A dance of light, a love so bold.

Moments linger, sweet and slow,
In starlit depths, our spirits grow.
With every touch, we find our place,
In layers of time, we trace our grace.

As constellations softly burn,
We hold each other, heartbeats turn.
In this vast space, we dare to dream,
Through layers of touch, we find our gleam.

In Each Other's Orbits We Shine

Caught in the pull of ancient light,
As planets dance, our souls ignite.
Circling close, we fade and spark,
In each other's orbits, we leave our mark.

With gentle sway, we navigate,
The gravity of love, our fate.
Through cosmic storms and quiet nights,
In every glance, the world unites.

Whispers float on starlit waves,
In harmony, our essence saves.
Weave through the dark, a blazing trail,
Together strong, we will not fail.

In playful spins, our laughter sings,
In the silence, joy still clings.
Each moment shared, a star reborn,
In endless circles, we are sworn.

Side by side, we journey far,
The universe our guiding star.
Together we dance, forever entwined,
In each other's orbits, true love defined.

The Fabric of Us Unfurled

Threads of time, stitched with care,
Woven moments, laid out bare.
Patterns form from joy and pain,
The fabric of us, in sunlight rain.

Colors blend in twilight glow,
Every hue tells what we know.
Underneath the vast skies blue,
We find a strength in me and you.

With every tear, a patch is sewn,
In laughter's warmth, our seeds are grown.
Together bold, we share the thread,
In every mark, the love we've bred.

Each knot we tie, a memory spun,
The fabric shines, we are as one.
In tapestry, our spirits blend,
A story written without end.

As seasons change, we rearrange,
The fabric of us, never strange.
Through stormy skies and sunny days,
In love's embrace, our hearts ablaze.

Where Heartbeats Meet

In the silence, our rhythms blend,
Two gentle pulses, a sweet transcend.
Between the beats, a language flows,
Whispered secrets the heart knows.

In crowded rooms, we feel the pull,
While the world spins, our hearts are full.
A simple glance, a touch divine,
Where heartbeats meet, the stars align.

Moments shared, like fleeting dreams,
In waves of love, our spirit gleams.
Through tangled thoughts and silent prayer,
In the dance of life, we find our care.

Through every sigh, our souls connect,
In every touch, we self-reflect.
A symphony of love, pure and sweet,
In this sacred space, where heartbeats meet.

Together strong, we draw our breath,
In unity, we conquer death.
Through all that's real and all that's true,
Where heartbeats meet, it's me and you.

The Pulse of Shared Dreams

In twilight's embrace, we weave our hopes,
Silent whispers linger, as night gently copes.
Stars above sparkle, our wishes take flight,
Bound by the dreams that ignite in the night.

Together we stand, with hearts intertwined,
In the dance of our souls, a rhythm aligned.
Through every heartbeat, our visions converge,
The pulse of our dreams begins to emerge.

In laughter and tears, we chase the unknown,
Each step a promise, together we've grown.
In every shared glance, in every soft sigh,
The pulse of our dreams will never say goodbye.

In moments of stillness, we find our way,
Through shadows and light, we choose to stay.
For in the canvas of life, we both paint,
A masterpiece formed, where love cannot faint.

As dawn breaks anew, our dreams soar high,
In unity's strength, we reach for the sky.
With each heartbeat echoed, a testament clear,
The pulse of our shared dreams will always be near.

In the Reflective Pool of Each Other

In still waters deep, reflections align,
Your eyes hold the secrets that are so divine.
A gaze that speaks volumes, without a word said,
In the pool of your essence, I see the thread.

With every soft ripple, our truths start to blend,
Mirrored emotions, a story we send.
Each flicker of light on the surface so clear,
In the depth of our souls, I recognize fear.

The world may be noisy, but here it is calm,
In each other's presence, we find our balm.
A tranquil embrace where silence unfolds,
In the reflective pool, our hearts become bold.

In laughter and sorrow, we float hand in hand,
The waters, our canvas where dreams gently stand.
Together we dive beneath the surface so true,
In the reflective pool, it's just me and you.

With every shared moment, the connection runs deep,
In the pool of our hearts, we silently keep.
A world of reflection, where love knows no end,
In the mirror of each other, we endlessly blend.

Shadows of Love in Sunlight

Under golden rays, our silhouettes sway,
In the warmth of your laughter, I find my way.
Shadows dancing softly, a gentle embrace,
Love's light surrounds us, a sacred space.

With every step forward, the shadows grow long,
Yet together in sunlight, our spirits are strong.
We chase fleeting moments, with joy and delight,
Through shadows of love, we linger in light.

The whispers of breezes, the warmth of the day,
In stillness and motion, we both choose to stay.
Each glance a reminder, with hearts open wide,
In the shadows of love, we never divide.

As the sun starts to set, painting skies gold,
In the warmth of our bond, there's a story untold.
Together we journey, no distances far,
In the shadows of love, we shine like a star.

With every sunset's glow, our love's anthem plays,
In shadows together, we dance through the haze.
For in unity's heart, we find our own song,
Shadows of love in sunlight, where we both belong.

As Close as a Breath Apart

In the silence of night, your heartbeat I hear,
A rhythm so close, it drives away fear.
With each gentle whisper, in dreams we confide,
As close as a breath, in love, we abide.

The space between moments, a sacred embrace,
In the warmth of your presence, I always find grace.
Through shadows and laughter, together we chart,
A journey of souls, as close as a heart.

In the flutter of leaves, in the whispers of rain,
Our spirits entwined, we share joy and pain.
With every soft sigh, we play our sweet part,
In the dance of existence, as close as a heart.

The universe spins, yet we stand so near,
In the depths of your gaze, I have nothing to fear.
Through the ebb and the flow, we'll never depart,
As close as a breath, forever we start.

With dreams intertwined, our paths gently meet,
In the arms of each other, we find our own beat.
With each step we take, we're never apart,
As close as a breath, united in heart.

Bathed in Shared Glances

In a crowded room we meet,
Eyes connect, a silent greet.
Words unspoken, warmth ablaze,
Lost in those enchanting rays.

Moments linger, hearts align,
With each glance, our souls entwine.
Time stands still, the world fades,
Together, in this sweet charade.

A gentle smile, a fleeting sigh,
Underneath the same vast sky.
In this sphere of tender light,
Bathed in glances, pure delight.

Unveiled secrets, whispered dreams,
In the silence, our heart gleams.
Connected by the sweetest chance,
We're lost within this dance.

As the evening drifts away,
In our eyes, the night will stay.
For in those glances exchanged,
A universe is arranged.

Beneath a Canopy of Dreams

Under stars, our spirits soar,
A tapestry of dreams galore.
Whispers float on evening air,
In this moment, nothing compares.

The moonlight casts a silver hue,
As visions of the night come true.
Together we chase the sublime,
Bound by hope, transcending time.

In the shadows, laughter blooms,
Filling up the filled-up rooms.
Hearts awaken, soft and free,
Beneath this sky, just you and me.

Each wish we weave brings us near,
In this refuge we hold dear.
Nestled close in the midnight beams,
Forever bound in shared dreams.

As dawn approaches, light will break,
Yet in this realm, we won't forsake.
For under skies that always gleam,
We've built a lasting dream.

The Dance of Shared Solitude

In a world that feels so vast,
We find solace in the past.
Two souls drifting side by side,
In stillness, our hearts confide.

Wrapped in silence, time suspends,
In quietude, the spirit mends.
Each breath a pulse, a soft refrain,
Together here, we break the chain.

The shadows whisper, secrets flow,
In shared solitude, we grow.
Beneath the weight of our embrace,
We've carved out our sacred space.

A gentle nod, a knowing glance,
In this stillness, there's romance.
Two bodies move, without a sound,
In solitude, connection found.

As night unfolds its velvet shroud,
We revel in the quiet crowd.
For in this dance, we've come to see,
Solitude's gentle harmony.

Merging Worlds in a Gentle Embrace

Two lives intersect like streams,
Fusing paths, fulfilling dreams.
In the cradle of the night,
We find comfort, pure delight.

With every touch, our borders blur,
In this moment, hearts confer.
Worlds collide, yet softly flow,
Boundless love begins to grow.

In the warmth of your tender gaze,
I am lost within a haze.
Gentle whispers, secrets shared,
In this dance, we've both prepared.

As the stars begin to weep,
In our arms, the universe sleeps.
Merging worlds, a sweet embrace,
In this haven, find our place.

Tomorrow's light may call us back,
Yet in dreams, we'll stay on track.
Together here, come what may,
In this love, we'll forever stay.

Tender Threads of Connection

In a world where silence speaks,
We find our hearts entwined,
A gentle touch ignites the flame,
In tender threads, love is defined.

Eyes that meet across the room,
A spark that travels far and wide,
With every glance, a deeper bond,
In quiet strength, we take our stride.

Laughter dances in the air,
The warmth of friendship's embrace,
Through life's tangled, winding roads,
We weave a timeless, sacred space.

Hands held tight through stormy nights,
A promise made beneath the skies,
Together we face the unknown,
With hope that lifts and never dies.

In the tapestry of our days,
Each moment stitched with care,
We treasure what brings us close,
In connection, love laid bare.

Whispered Secrets Beneath the Stars

Beneath a blanket of the night,
We share our dreams and fears,
The cosmos listens, ever proud,
As whispered truths dance in our ears.

Stars twinkle like knowing eyes,
While shadows cradle tender sighs,
Each secret told, a wish released,
In the stillness, our hearts fly high.

The moon, a witness to our tales,
Bathes us in its silver glow,
With every breath, we forge a bond,
In this celestial "yes" we know.

Time slows down, the world fades out,
As we share the vast unknown,
Beneath this sky, our spirits blend,
In whispered dreams, we find our home.

So let the night hold our secrets,
As constellations softly gleam,
For in the dark, true magic lies,
In whispered secrets, we dare to dream.

In the Arms of Quietude

In silent moments, calm and pure,
We find our solace, sweet release,
The world fades softly, hushed and still,
In quietude, we taste our peace.

A gentle breeze whispers our names,
The leaves respond with soft embrace,
Nestled in nature's tender hold,
We lose ourselves in the still space.

With every breath, our worries slip,
Like ripples fading on the shore,
In tranquility, our hearts align,
In the arms of stillness, we restore.

So let us linger in this grace,
Where time stands still, a sacred gift,
In the arms of quietude, we find,
An infinite place where spirits lift.

Embraced by silence, fears dissolve,
In rapture of this gentle sound,
In tranquil dreams, we drift away,
In the arms of peace, we are unbound.

Soft Echoes of Heartbeats

In the hush of a fading day,
Soft echoes beat and intertwine,
Each pulse a rhythm, tender song,
In quiet moments, love's design.

With every heartbeat, stories bloom,
A symphony of hope and grace,
As time flows gently like a stream,
In soft reflections, we find our place.

Eyes that sparkle, whispers low,
In this sacred dance of souls,
Every echo speaks of warmth,
In heartbeats shared, love unfurls.

We hold each other close and tight,
As shadows blend with evening light,
In these embraces, life reveals,
The beauty found in love's delight.

So listen closely, hearts in tune,
Together singing, hearts combined,
In soft echoes, we are alive,
In every heartbeat, love defined.

The Warmth of Mutual Knowing

In laughter shared, our hearts align,
A bond that glows, like sunlit wine.
Each secret whispered, gently laid,
In the cradle of trust, love won't fade.

Through trials faced, we stand as one,
In shadows cast, we find our sun.
With every glance, a truth unfolds,
Our spirits dance as warmth enfolds.

In silence felt, connections grow,
In every touch, pure feelings flow.
An unspoken pact, forever tight,
In deepest knowing, we find our light.

Through shared moments, the world grows small,
In your embrace, I feel it all.
In tender whispers, we will find,
The warmth of mutual knowing, so kind.

And as the years weave golden threads,
In every laugh, and sorrow shed.
Together we rise, like tides that swell,
Bound by the stories we both tell.

When Souls Gaze Without Words

Eyes meet softly, the silence sings,
In a world apart, our spirit clings.
Every glance a tale, unspoken yet clear,
In the depths of your gaze, I see what's dear.

No need for voices, our hearts converse,
In the quiet space, we feel the universe.
Like leaves on the breeze, our souls intertwine,
In moments like these, all things align.

With every heartbeat, we share a song,
In the stillness, where we belong.
A touch of your hand, a soft embrace,
In that gentle warmth, we find our place.

When souls gaze deeply, the world fades away,
In the brilliance of love, we choose to stay.
In the tapestry woven, a bond so tight,
Our hearts together, pure and bright.

As dusk turns to dawn and shadows wane,
In this quiet space, there's no more pain.
Just the rhythm of trust, endlessly spun,
In the gaze of our souls, eternally one.

Nestled in Harmonious Silence

In the hush of the night, we find our peace,
A tranquil heart where voices cease.
With every breath, the world stands still,
Nestled in silence, we feel the thrill.

The stars above, they quietly gleam,
In moments shared, we softly dream.
Wrapped in warmth, our spirits soar,
Together we linger, wanting more.

A soothing calm, where tender hearts meet,
In silence profound, our souls feel complete.
In the whisper of leaves and the moon's gentle glow,
We find the love that we both know.

In this sacred space, no words are required,
In the depth of your gaze, my heart's inspired.
Through timeless moments, we softly dance,
Nestled in harmony, lost in romance.

The clock stands still, as time fades away,
In this gentle hush, we forever stay.
Love flows like water, serene and clear,
In harmonious silence, I hold you near.

The Beauty of Being Known

In a world of facades, you see my heart,
In the beauty of knowing, we've made a start.
With every laugh and tear shared,
In the depths of your gaze, I feel bared.

Through stories and dreams, we weave our tale,
In the softness of love, we shall not fail.
Each moment cherished, like petals that bloom,
In the garden of trust, our hearts resume.

With every heartbeat, the connection grows,
In the dance of our spirits, true beauty flows.
When the night falls and shadows creep,
In the light of your knowing, my soul can weep.

In the embrace of acceptance, I find my place,
My heart laid open, a tender space.
In the beauty of being known, I feel free,
With you by my side, just let it be.

So here we stand, against the tide,
In the strength of our bond, forever tied.
Through all of life's storms, we shall remain,
In the beauty of knowing, there's no more pain.

Sculpture of Silent Affection

In the stillness, whispers trace,
Chiseled love in quiet grace.
Hands that mold the softest clay,
Crafting dreams in bright array.

Time stands still in tender hold,
A story formed that's yet untold.
Heartbeats echo through the stone,
In the silence, love is grown.

Chiseled shadows, light and shade,
Every curve, a promise laid.
Fingers dance, emotions flow,
In silent work, true love will show.

The sculpture stands, a work divine,
Emotions caught in every line.
A timeless piece forever cast,
In silent praise, affection lasts.

Nature breathes in every part,
Art combined with human heart.
In this stillness, we both find,
A sculpture of the soul aligned.

Poetics of Proximity

In the hush where hearts align,
Space dissolves, your hand in mine.
Quiet glances, soft and pure,
In this closeness, we endure.

Fleeting moments intertwine,
Words unspoken, eyes align.
Close enough to feel the spark,
In the light, we chase the dark.

Every breath, a whispered thought,
In your smile, I am caught.
Distance fades in the night's embrace,
Poetry found in this place.

With each heartbeat, rhythms flow,
In the silence, feelings grow.
A dance of souls beneath the sky,
In this proximity, we fly.

As stars twinkle, dreams take flight,
Closer still, we hold on tight.
In this universe, we are one,
Poetics written, love begun.

The Thread That Binds

Invisible, yet strong and true,
A golden thread connects us two.
Through all trials, we hold tight,
Woven hearts in day and night.

Each moment stitches memories grand,
With every laugh, with every hand.
Across the miles, we still reside,
The thread that binds will be our guide.

In laughter shared and sorrows sown,
Through ups and downs, we've always grown.
A tapestry of love displayed,
In every hue, our lives portrayed.

Through storms that rage and sunlit days,
The thread endures through all our ways.
A bond so deep, it won't unwind,
Forever joined, our hearts combined.

With every twist, the fabric glows,
In unity, our story flows.
A thread of love, forever bright,
The ties we cherish, pure delight.

Sunshine in the Shadows

When daylight dims and shadows creep,
In darkened corners, secrets seep.
Yet through the gloom, a warmth can shine,
A glimmer where our hopes entwine.

With every dusk, a promise made,
In quiet moments, fears do fade.
A flicker bright in muted hues,
The light within, we choose to use.

In shadows cast by fleeting time,
We find a rhythm, a gentle rhyme.
Like sunbeams breaking through the gray,
Love finds a path to light the way.

The dance of dusk and dawn's embrace,
In every struggle, we find grace.
Though shadows linger, hope remains,
A sunflower blooming after rains.

In the silence, glow and gleam,
Creating light from every dream.
Together we will face the night,
With sunshine found in each delight.

The Space Between Words

In quiet moments, silence speaks,
A whisper lingers, heart still seeks.
The pause tells tales of what we know,
In every gap, deep feelings flow.

Each heartbeat echoes, softly spins,
In every sigh, a story begins.
The air between us holds our breath,
With every glance, we flirt with depth.

Meaning blooms in the empty air,
In that stillness, love feels rare.
What's unsaid softly writes the part,
The space between, a beating heart.

Words may falter, but hearts align,
In that space, your hand finds mine.
Unvoiced wishes dance and play,
In silence, love finds its way.

Treasures of Tenderness

Softly spoken, gentle touch,
In simple acts, we learn so much.
A warm embrace, a knowing smile,
These treasures linger all the while.

In kindness found in every day,
Building bridges where hearts can sway.
A tender glance, a friendly nod,
These little gifts, our lives applaud.

In moments shared, our spirits soar,
With every laugh, we're rich in lore.
Collecting gems, both rare and sweet,
In the smallest things, our joys complete.

Through trials faced, we give, we share,
In the harshness, find love's care.
We treasure warmth, connection true,
In tenderness, our hearts renew.

Merging Paths

Two roads converge in morning light,
A meeting place, we feel it right.
Steps once solo, now intertwine,
In this moment, your soul meets mine.

A shared journey, hand in hand,
Together we weave, make our stand.
With open hearts and dreams held high,
We chase the stars across the sky.

Unfolding stories, side by side,
In this adventure, we take pride.
Every twist brings us more near,
United voices, we shall cheer.

Though paths may stray, and seasons change,
Our hearts remain, they'll never range.
In every turn, I'll find my way,
The bond we share won't ever sway.

Timeless Glances

In fleeting moments, worlds collide,
With every look, love's truth can't hide.
A timeless glance can light the way,
In silent vows, our hearts will stay.

Across the years, our eyes meet,
In memories, the past is sweet.
Each gaze a promise, pure and bright,
In every sparkle, there's a light.

Through whispered words and laughter shared,
In those glances, every heart bared.
A knowing nod, a spark ignites,
As time stands still, the soul alights.

No need for words, when eyes converse,
A dance of souls, the universe.
In timeless glances, love's embrace,
We find our home in this shared space.

A Mosaic of Shared Moments

In laughter's echo, we find our truth,
The light of joy, in fleeting youth.
Memories blend in colors bright,
Each moment crafted, pure delight.

Hand in hand, we dance through time,
With every heartbeat, lives intertwine.
The tapestry grows, stitch by stitch,
A bond unbroken, a sacred niche.

Whispers of hopes under the stars,
Mapping our dreams, no distance far.
In silence shared, our spirits soar,
Across the canvas, forevermore.

Fragments of days in gentle sweep,
In the hours we cherish, love runs deep.
A mosaic filled with vibrant hues,
A masterpiece of me and you.

Through changing seasons, we still hold tight,
Finding comfort in shared twilight.
Together woven, a timeless thread,
In this cherished space, we are led.

Touchstones of Our Togetherness

Beneath the canopy of stars so bright,
We carve our names in the soft twilight.
Every shared glance, a story unfolds,
Touchstones that sparkle, memories bold.

In laughter's embrace, we find our way,
In gentle whispers, our hearts sway.
Moments like feathers, light and free,
Together we flourish, just you and me.

Through every storm, we rise and shine,
With hands entwined, our fates align.
A garden of trust, blooms in our deeds,
As we nurture love, sowing its seeds.

In the soft glow of dusk, we reflect,
On the paths we've walked, the lives we've checked.
Each touch and smile, a sacred bond,
In the tapestry of life, we're fond.

The essence of us, woven like lace,
In each heartbeat shared, we find our place.
Together we stand, come what may,
Our touchstones guide us, day by day.

The Essence of Cherished Connection

In the depths of silence, our hearts converse,
In the glow of dawn, we feel the universe.
Every shared look, a quiet embrace,
The essence we feel, no one can replace.

A dance of souls in intricate flow,
The bond that we share continues to grow.
Through the laughter and tears, we remain,
A sanctuary built from love's sweet refrain.

We carve our paths, side by side,
In the waves of time, we firmly glide.
In every heartbeat, a symphony plays,
A melody wrapped in the warmth of days.

With each moment lived, our spirits entwine,
In the fabric of love, we gently dine.
The essence of us, a fragrant bloom,
Filling the air, dispelling the gloom.

Like threads of gold in the quiet night,
Together we shine—oh, so bright!
A beautiful dance, will forever flow,
The essence of connection, marked by glow.

Weaving Stories with Silken Threads

In the loom of life, we spin our tale,
Each thread a whisper, soft as a gale.
Stories entwined in vibrant hue,
Weaving our dreams, both old and new.

With laughter's stitch and love's embrace,
We navigate time, at our own pace.
In tapestry rich, our lives come alive,
Making our home where memories thrive.

Every moment shared, a silken weave,
In the heart's design, we believe.
Stitched with the hopes that softly gleam,
Together we create our common dream.

Through seasons of change, our threads remain,
In the fabric of life, we dance through pain.
With needles of joy, we mend and create,
A story of love that will never abate.

So let's gather round, share tales anew,
In this woven world, it's me and you.
Weaving together, a magical thread,
A tapestry rich, where love's gently spread.

The Art of Being Close

In whispers soft, we find our way,
A gentle touch at close of day.
Hearts aligned, we softly beat,
In every moment, love runs sweet.

The world fades out, it's just us two,
In silence shared, we feel what's true.
Connected souls, we dance as one,
The art of being close, pure fun.

With every glance, a secret told,
In warmth and trust, our dreams unfold.
Breath of togetherness fills the air,
In this embrace, we shed all care.

Through tangled paths, we make our way,
In harmony, we choose to stay.
Together here, our fears dispelled,
The art of being close, we meld.

For in this space, all shadows part,
In every laugh, you hold my heart.
With every smile, we spark the light,
In closeness found, we greet the night.

In Shared Laughter

When laughter spills like sunshine bright,
It dances in the air, pure delight.
With every chuckle, joy expands,
A symphony made by sun-kissed hands.

In playful jests, we weave our bond,
Through silly tales, of which we're fond.
The world grows light as we take flight,
With every giggle, hearts ignite.

In crowded rooms or quiet nooks,
Our laughter shines like open books.
We share our dreams, our hopes, our fears,
In every laugh, we dry our tears.

Through trials faced, we find our grace,
In friendly jests, we leave our trace.
Together, faced with life's demands,
United in laughter, hand in hands.

In every moment, joy unfurls,
A melody that colors worlds.
In shared laughter, we take flight,
Bound by joy, we light the night.

Our Spirits Soar

With open hearts, we touch the skies,
In dreams that lift, where passion flies.
Through every step, our spirits rise,
In this sweet dance, love never lies.

We chase the dawn, we greet the stars,
Through distant lands, and still so far.
In whispered words, and glances shared,
We find the strength, our souls prepared.

In laughter's breeze, our worries fade,
Through wooded paths, in light and shade.
Together strong, we break the chains,
Our spirits soar, in joy's refrains.

In every sunrise, in every moon,
Our hearts are basing their own tune.
Through storms and trials, we hold fast,
With hope and love, we'll always last.

In vibrant dreams, our spirits soar,
In endless peace, we yearn for more.
With every breath, and every sigh,
Together here, we learn to fly.

Hidden Journeys of the Heart

In quiet corners, secrets dwell,
In whispers soft, their stories swell.
Through gentle paths, the heart will roam,
In these hidden journeys, we find home.

With every tear, a lesson learned,
In love's embrace, our passions burned.
Through shadowed doubts and bold confessions,
We navigate the heart's obsessions.

The softest sigh, a silent plea,
In every pulse, we crave to be.
In distant dreams, where hopes entwine,
Hidden journeys shaped by time.

Through winding roads, we journey on,
In every dusk, a brand new dawn.
With every heartbeat, every scar,
The hidden journeys take us far.

In depths of night, we search for light,
In every heartbeat, purest sight.
Together, we find paths that start,
Through hidden journeys of the heart.

Together, We Please the Night

As twilight falls, we greet the stars,
In whispered dreams, and visions ours.
Through softened glow, the world ignites,
Together here, we please the night.

In every laugh, a spark begins,
We dance through shadows, where love wins.
With gentle steps, we find our way,
Together, we embrace the sway.

The moonlight bathes our souls in grace,
With every glance, we find our place.
In harmony, the night unfolds,
Together hearts, as love beholds.

With every heartbeat, we create,
A magic that we celebrate.
In every moment, our spirits ignite,
Together, we please the night.

In whispered dreams, we share our fears,
Through starlit skies, and joyful cheers.
Together, side by side, we light,
A radiant flame, as we please the night.

Whispers in the Night

Moonlight dances on the ground,
Silent secrets all around.
Stars are blinking, soft and bright,
Carrying dreams into the night.

Shadows flicker, shapes appear,
Echoes of a voice so clear.
In the stillness, hearts ignite,
And find solace in the night.

Gentle breezes brush the trees,
Telling tales with every breeze.
With a sigh, the world takes flight,
Finding peace in whispered light.

Voices mingle, laughter's glow,
In this hush, time moves slow.
Underneath the starry height,
We make wishes, hold on tight.

When the dawn begins to creep,
Memories of night, we keep.
Holding softly what feels right,
In the magic of the night.

Heartbeats Entwined

Two souls dance in gentle sway,
Stepping close in warm ballet.
Heartbeat whispers, soft and true,
Creating rhythms just for two.

Time stands still, the world fades,
In their eyes, the love cascades.
Every touch, a silent vow,
In this moment, here and now.

Fingers brush, igniting fire,
Building dreams, deep desire.
With each heartbeat, hearts align,
A symphony, so divine.

Between the breaths, a sacred space,
Where every heartbeat finds its place.
In the quiet, love defines,
The magic of two heartbeats entwined.

And as the stars begin to fade,
Promises linger, love remade.
In every pulse, they intertwine,
Forever bound, hearts aligned.

The Language of Fingers

Fingers dance on whispered strings,
Crafting dreams and secret things.
In the silence, stories flow,
Each caress, a tale to show.

Tracing paths upon the skin,
Telling stories held within.
Every touch, a gentle hint,
Of love's language, soft and mint.

Delicate as morning dew,
Shaping worlds in every hue.
In the stillness, they align,
Speaking softly, hearts combine.

Through the night, the fingers glide,
In this dance, they will abide.
With every pull and gentle twist,
They create a bond, a loving tryst.

When dawn breaks, and shadows flee,
This language holds eternity.
In every touch, love's design,
Written sweetly, divine intertwine.

Beneath the Softest Skin

Whispers breathe in night's embrace,
Underneath the tender space.
Secrets lie, a hidden grin,
Found within the softest skin.

Gentle warmth, a quiet sway,
Every heartbeat, a sweet ballet.
In shadows deep, where dreams begin,
Lies the truth beneath the skin.

Touching gently, tracing light,
Easing worries of the night.
In this bond, they find their kin,
Woven tight beneath the skin.

With every laugh, and every sigh,
Moments linger, time slips by.
In every pulse, they feel the spin,
A dance of love beneath the skin.

As dawn unfolds with golden thread,
They will carry what's been said.
Holding close where love has been,
Forever held beneath the skin.

The Gentle Tug of Familiar Souls

In quiet corners we find our way,
A glance exchanged, words left to play.
Threads of connection softly weave,
In the heart's tapestry, we believe.

Through shared laughter and silent sighs,
We dance beneath the endless skies.
In every memory, a story told,
A gentle tug, a bond to hold.

Like whispers echoing in the night,
Familiar souls share their light.
In the comfort of our gentle grace,
Together we find our sacred space.

With every heartbeat, trust is grown,
In the warmth of love we've known.
We navigate the depths unknown,
Hand in hand, we're never alone.

At twilight's balm, we rest our dreams,
In the flow of life's quiet streams.
The world fades, we take our flight,
In the embrace of endless night.

Our Secrets Carried by the Wind

Beneath the sky so vast and wide,
Whispers linger, a silent guide.
Secrets danced on the breeze so sweet,
In every sigh, our souls discreet.

Through rustling leaves and swaying trees,
We share our dreams with the gentle breeze.
A song of hope, a tale of time,
Every secret wrapped in rhyme.

The wind will carry what hearts must say,
In the warm glow of the fading day.
In its arms, our voices roam,
A tether to the world we call home.

From mountain peaks to ocean's edge,
Our words are woven, a sacred pledge.
Though oceans may rise, and storms may bend,
Our secrets remain, a timeless trend.

In every gust, truth finds its way,
In the dance of dusk, in the light of day.
We trust the wind to guard our lore,
A vessel of trust, forevermore.

The Heart's Hidden Haven

In a corner quiet, still, and bright,
The heart finds solace, a sacred sight.
Nestled deep where shadows play,
A hidden haven to drift away.

Amidst the chaos, it softly calls,
A calm refuge within these walls.
Here, dreams take root and gently bloom,
In tender whispers, dispelling gloom.

With every breath, we carve the space,
For love's embrace, a warm grace.
In laughter soft and tears that flow,
The heart's hidden place begins to grow.

A sanctuary built on trust,
Where moments linger, love is a must.
Within its depths, we lay our fears,
In the cradle of hope, wipe away tears.

Here, every heartbeat sings its tune,
A melody whispered beneath the moon.
In this haven, pure and true,
The heart finds peace; I find you.

Stitches of Affection Beneath the Surface

In quiet stitches, love is sewn,
Each thread a bond we have grown.
Beneath the surface, where we reside,
Affection's fabric does not hide.

The tales we weave in moments shared,
With gentle hands, both kind and spared.
In every touch, a story told,
In warmth and care, our hearts unfold.

Through life's fabric, we find our way,
In laughter's echo, in shadows' play.
Each stitch a memory, fragile yet strong,
In the quilt of belonging, we belong.

Though storms may come and seasons change,
Our stitches remain, forever strange.
In the patterns we form, love takes flight,
A comforting blanket against the night.

Together we'll patch the ragged seams,
In the warmth of shared, woven dreams.
With threads of gold binding us near,
In this tapestry, we conquer fear.

The Art of Being Near

A silent glance, a knowing sigh,
Hearts entwined, with no need to try.
In the stillness, we find our way,
Side by side, come what may.

Soft whispers dance upon the breeze,
In your presence, my soul's at ease.
Each moment shared, a treasure to hold,
In the warmth, love's stories unfold.

Through shadows cast and light that beams,
Together we weave our tender dreams.
In closeness, we discover life's song,
With every heartbeat, we belong.

The art of being, pure and true,
In every smile, I see me and you.
Let the world fade, let time stand still,
In this silence, I feel your will.

In the flicker of stars, our laughter glows,
In this embrace, affection flows.
Here's to the beauty of life's gentle cheer,
Bound forever, the art of being near.

Unraveled Secrets

Whispers hidden in shadows dark,
A tale unfolds with a single spark.
Secrets linger like leaves in fall,
Tales of truth, in shadows call.

Quiet moments unmask the past,
In shared silence, bonds are cast.
With each stitch, the fabric breaks,
The heart reveals what it aches.

In the twilight, mysteries rise,
Beneath the surface, beauty lies.
Unearth the layers, let love steer,
In vulnerability, we have no fear.

Truth dances lightly on the tongue,
Within our hearts, a song is sung.
Trust the journey, embrace the cracks,
In the unspoken, love never lacks.

Unraveled secrets, soft and bright,
In the darkness, we find the light.
Together we wander, hand in hand,
In the realm of trust, we shall stand.

Unity in Vulnerability

In the cracks of our shining masks,
Lies the truth that love always asks.
To be seen, to be known most real,
In shared weakness, strength we feel.

With open hearts, we gather close,
In tender moments, we become engrossed.
Fragile threads weave stories bold,
In our honesty, warmth unfolds.

Let the walls we build fall away,
In rawness, we discover the fray.
Each scar shared is a story told,
In unity found, we become whole.

In the space where fears reside,
We hold the shadows and confide.
In the tender embrace of the unknown,
With courage found, we are shown.

Together we dance on this fragile line,
In vulnerability, our hearts align.
With every breath, we redefine,
The beauty within, a bond divine.

Kindred Spirits in Stillness

In the hush of dawn's soft light,
Two souls meet, a beautiful sight.
With quiet hearts, we softly breathe,
In stillness, our spirits weave.

The world fades to a gentle hum,
In this moment, we've both come.
Every glance, a silent farewell,
In the calm, our stories dwell.

Nature whispers to our hearts,
From discord, we embrace the parts.
In every pause, a bond flows free,
The art of stillness sings to me.

With open arms, we share the space,
In our silence, we find our grace.
Kindred spirits, forever near,
In this stillness, love is clear.

As time drifts by, we remain still,
Two hearts echoing a shared will.
Together in peace, we shall exist,
In the beauty of moments, not to be missed.

Intimate Conversations with the Moon

Beneath the silver glow we meet,
Whispers of secrets softly greet.
The stars listen to our shared sighs,
In this dance, our hearts arise.

Each shadow stretches, a gentle caress,
The night air wraps us in its dress.
In silence, our spirits intertwine,
A fleeting moment, forever divine.

Moonlight spills on your soft skin,
In this stillness, dreams begin.
With every glance, the universe bends,
In whispers eternal, love transcends.

We carve our stories on the night sky,
Echoes of laughter, each time we try.
The moon holds secrets not meant to fade,
Intimate conversations serenely made.

As dawn approaches, the light encroaches,
Yet still, our bond never broaches.
In shadows, our hearts shall stay tuned,
With every moonrise, a love renewed.

Unraveled Threads of Connection

In gentle whispers, we find our way,
Through tangled paths where shadows play.
Each heartbeat a rhythm, a song anew,
In silence, two souls merge as one true.

Fingers trace maps on worn-out skin,
A tapestry woven where love begins.
Each stitch a reminder, each knot a plea,
In this space, we are bound, we are free.

Through laughter and tears, the fabric wears thin,
Yet stronger we stand, our spirits akin.
The world may tug, but we hold tight,
In this connection, we find our light.

Like threads of fate, woven and spun,
In every challenge, we've already won.
In twilight's whisper, our spirits entwine,
Unraveled, yet whole, forever divine.

With every dawn, new patterns arise,
A dance of connection beneath open skies.
In this tapestry, love's colors blend,
Unraveled threads, where beginnings transcend.

The Softness of a Shared Breath

In quiet moments, we gaze in awe,
The world fades softly, without a flaw.
Breaths intertwine, a rhythm so deep,
In this space, every secret we keep.

Your presence, a balm to a weary soul,
In soft whispers, we become whole.
With every exhale, the barrier falls,
In this exchange, the heart gently calls.

Eyes closed, we drift in the gentle tide,
Floating in stillness, where feelings abide.
Each shared breath, an ethereal blend,
In these moments, we truly transcend.

Time stretches, the universe bends,
In the soft silence, our meaning extends.
As stars watch over this sacred trust,
In shared breaths, our love is a must.

When the world awakens, noise will intrude,
But in this soft moment, forever renewed.
In shared breaths, find the essence of grace,
Together we flourish in this sacred space.

Gentle Ignition of Hearts

A spark ignites in tender embrace,
Two wandering souls find their place.
With every glance, a fire ignites,
In your smile, the universe lights.

The warmth of connection, soft and slow,
A dance of flames in the ebb and flow.
Together we flicker, together we blaze,
In quiet moments, lost in a gaze.

Amidst the chaos, we rise above,
In the gentle ignition, we find our love.
Every whisper fuels the flame,
Each heartbeat, a new, wild name.

As embers shimmer and dare to soar,
In the quiet night, our spirits pour.
A tapestry of warmth wrapped tight,
In the gentle ignition of heart's pure light.

Through storms and shadows, we bravely tread,
With every heartbeat, love's thread is fed.
Together, in this luminous art,
We cherish the gentle ignition of hearts.

Unscripted Moments of Togetherness

In laughter's embrace, we find our way,
Through the wild paths of our fleeting day.
With every glance, a story unfolds,
In this dance of life, our hearts are bold.

A whispered secret beneath the stars,
Moments unplanned, like Jupiter and Mars.
We share the silence, a comfortable space,
In the rhythm of souls, we find our place.

Time pauses gently, as we hold on tight,
To fragments of joy, in the soft twilight.
Each heartbeat together, a precious sound,
In the chaos of life, our haven is found.

Through time's swift current, we drift and sway,
Each unscripted moment, a new holiday.
In the echoes of laughter, we weave our dreams,
Together forever, or so it seems.

And when shadows fall, and day turns to night,
We cherish the warmth, that feels just right.
In unscripted moments, love thrives and grows,
A journey together, where anything goes.

Tangled in the Warmth of Us

In twilight's glow, we find our way,
Wrapped in laughter, come what may.
Fingers entwined, like roots of a tree,
In the warmth of our love, we are free.

The world blurs away, as we dance slow,
In each other's arms, all fears let go.
With the heartbeat of night, we forge our fate,
In this timeless embrace, we celebrate.

Through tangled paths and winding roads,
Together we carry our shared loads.
Even in storms, our light will shine,
In the tangled warmth, your heart is mine.

Moments like fireflies, flicker and gleam,
In the lush of the night, we live our dream.
Every glance, a promise, every touch, a song,
In this wondrous dance, where we belong.

So let's twirl through the night, beneath the moon's glow,
In the warmth of our love, let the passion flow.
With every heartbeat, we write our tale,
In the beauty of us, we will never fail.

The Gentle Ties that Bind

In quiet corners, our whispers blend,
Threads of connection that grasp and bend.
Through laughter and tears, we gently weave,
The tapestry of moments, we choose to believe.

With every touch, an unspoken word,
Echoes of trust, that cannot be heard.
The gentle ties that bind us tight,
Illuminate shadows, turning dark to light.

In the simplest gestures, love finds its way,
Through the ordinary, we build our play.
A knowing smile, a fleeting glance,
In the gentle ties, we take our chance.

Through life's winding road, hand in hand,
With every step, together we stand.
A beacon of hope, in stormy weather,
In the gentle bonds, we shine forever.

So here's to the ties, both simple and grand,
The gentle whispers of a lifelong plan.
Together we blossom, through thick and thin,
In the fabric of love, forever we spin.

Beneath the Surface

In the depths of silence, secrets reside,
Where whispers of dreams become our guide.
Beneath the surface, emotions flow,
A current of feelings, we both know.

Fleeting moments, like shadows on walls,
In the still of the night, our heart softly calls.
With every tear, a story unfolds,
Beneath the surface, our truth is told.

In the dance of shadows, we find our grace,
Lost in the depths, we embrace the space.
Every glance exchanged, a deeper dive,
Beneath the surface, our spirits thrive.

Through storms and valleys, we brave our fate,
In the quiet depths, we contemplate.
With hands intertwined, we rise and fall,
Beneath the surface, we conquer all.

So let's explore the layers within,
In each heartbeat, let our journey begin.
For beneath the surface, our love will bloom,
A garden of stars, we'll collectively groom.

Heartbeats Collide

In the hush of a moment, our heartbeats collide,
A symphony found where memories abide.
In this tender dance, we lose all control,
With every pulse, you echo my soul.

Through the chaos of life, we find our song,
In harmony's grasp, where we both belong.
Each softly spoken word, a tender stroke,
In the rhythm of love, together we awoke.

With every heartbeat, the world fades away,
In this electric embrace, we choose to stay.
A spark in the night, igniting the morn,
In the orchestra of love, our hearts are reborn.

Through laughter and tears, we dance our fate,
In the duets of life, we celebrate.
Every heartbeat a promise, a vow so sweet,
In this vibrant pulse, we become complete.

So let's dance forever, heartbeats in sync,
In the flow of our love, we'll never shrink.
As time gently moves, and seasons unfold,
In this beautiful collision, our story is told.

Milton Keynes UK
Ingram Content Group UK Ltd.
UKHW021208261024
450281UK00007B/100

9 789916 891001